Dysfunctional Documents

A 12-Step Recovery Program
for User Documentation

Dysfunctional Documents

A 12-Step Recovery Program
for User Documentation

Kurt Ament

ISBN 978-3-00-068352-7

Cover art: Adobe Stock

Levels of Edit
www.levels-of-edit.com

Also by Kurt Ament:

Single Sourcing: Building Modular Documentation

Indexing: A Nuts-and-Bolts Guide for Technical Writers

dys·func·tion

n.

1 Abnormal or impaired functioning of a bodily system or organ

2 Failure to achieve or sustain a behavioral norm or expected condition, as in a social relationship

Contents

Contents

Figures

Tables

Foreword

This guide is based on a simple idea: quality can be quantified.

I first encountered this idea in the early 1990s in a certificate program in technical communication co-sponsored by the Society for Technical Communication and the University of California at Los Angeles. Mary Fran Buehler was giving a weekend workshop on *The Levels of Edit*, the classic editing handbook she co-authored with Robert Van Buhren in the 1970s at Jet Propulsion Laboratory.

TIP: *The copyright-free handbook is difficult to find in print, so I have posted an electronic version on my website (www.levels-of-edit.com).*

Buehler opened her workshop with an unequivocal statement: "Editing is a business." She explained that every aspect of the editing process can be quantified. Her conclusion defined my subsequent career: "Quality can be quantified."

The Levels of Edit identifies nine edit types, which it configures into five edit levels, or editing service packages. In the past half-century, this flexible structure has been customized at numerous companies around the world. The core idea of quantifiable quality has stood the test of time.

Dysfunctional Documents is an attempt to show technical writers, editors, and publication managers how to define and use edit types and levels to systematically ratchet up the quality of their user documentation. It explains how to re-use the lessons learned in that process to establish best practices, or writing guidelines, to improve the quality of future documents.

It is extremely helpful to illustrate each guideline with negative and positive examples from edited documents. Example-driven guidelines provide a fault-tolerant, scalable foundation for a consensual style guide, which, in turn, serves as the collective memory for writing and editing teams.

For the guidelines to be accepted, they must be put through a formal approval process. Why go to all that trouble? Because writers, editors, and managers are human. They are most likely to accept, follow, and enforce guidelines that they themselves develop, thereby taking their documents to the next level.

Dysfunctional Documents explains how to make all that happen, based on my own hands-on experience at leading companies in science and industry.

Kurt Ament
December 2020

About this guide

This hands-on guide shows you how to use edit types and levels to transform dysfunctional documents into healthy documents. It provides a flexible 12-step process to diagnose problems, develop treatments, and prevent relapses. And it explains how to create, maintain, enforce, and even automate consensual writing guidelines to keep your documents healthy.

Each step in the process identifies the roles of writers, editors, and managers. You can customize the process, as needed.

Audience

This guide is designed for anyone interested in improving document usability:

- **Writers**
  Technical writers who want editors to help them improve the usability of their documents, not just bleed red ink on hard copies of finished documents

- **Editors**
  Technical editors who want to trade in their red pens for a proactive role in the information development process, increasing the quality of documents from day one

- **Managers**
  Writing managers and managing editors who want to improve the usability of their publications, increase the productivity of their teams, and save time and money

- **Translators**
  Translators who want to work on documents that are written clearly in a consistent and predictable voice

- **Students**
  Students of technical communication who want to learn more about the human side of technical writing and editing as practiced in the real world

Even if you work alone, the guide outlines specific steps you can take to improve the usability of your documents.

Purpose

This guide has two integrated goals:

- **Immediate success**
  It shows how to diagnose and treat dysfunction in user documentation. It explains how writers and editors can work together to solve problems in specific documents and then convert those solutions into writing guidelines.

- **Continuing success**
  It shows how to prevent dysfunction from creeping back into user documentation by refining the edit process. It outlines the specific roles and responsibilities of writers, editors, and managers in improving document quality.

Organization

This guide is organized as follows:

- **Hitting bottom**
  How to identify common symptoms of team dysfunction, such as failed collaboration, oversight, and guidelines

- **Step 1. Acknowledge problems**
  How to identify acute and chronic problems with new, legacy, merged, and outsourced documentation

- **Step 2. Define edit types**
  How to customize the classic edit types in *The Levels of Edit* to match the specific needs of your team

- **Step 3. Define edit levels**
  How to define distinct edit levels, or editing service packages, that can be referenced in edit request forms

- **Step 4. Edit documents**
  How to identify document problems by edit type and distinguish between global and specific problems

- **Step 5. Write edit reports**
  How to develop reports that illustrate problems and solutions with examples from the document being edited

- **Step 6. Evaluate edit reports**
  How to evaluate edit suggestions and identify best practices as potential writing guidelines

- **Step 7. Propose guidelines**
  How to compile potential writing guidelines into proposals and distribute them to team leaders for evaluation

- **Step 8. Evaluate guidelines**
  How to establish a proposal review process, evaluate individual proposals, and verify proposal decisions

- **Step 9. Publish guidelines**
  How to compile approved guidelines into a style guide and distribute it to all team members

- **Step 10. Enforce guidelines**
  How to explain and illustrate pertinent guidelines in subsequent document edits and reports

- **Step 11. Update guidelines**
  How to implement practical guidelines, repeal impractical guidelines, and establish exceptions and priorities

- **Step 12. Automate guidelines**
  How to identify solutions for automation, set up a cross-functional team, and build guidelines into tools

- **Appendix A.** *The Levels of Edit*
  Link to an electronic copy of *The Levels of Edit* as well as screenshots and explanations of key concepts

- **Appendix B. Edit request forms**
  Guidelines for requesting edits as well as samples of corresponding electronic forms

- **Appendix C. Writing guidelines**
  Writing guidelines, with negative and positive examples, taken from style guides at real companies

- **Appendix D. Roles and responsibilities**
  Roles of writers, editors, and managers in collaboration, oversight, treatment, and prevention

The guide also contains a list of references and an index.

Hitting bottom

User documentation mirrors the teams that develop it. Teams that pull in different directions are incoherent. Incoherent teams develop incoherent, or dysfunctional, documents.

The first step in recovery is acknowledgement. The moment you acknowledge document dysfunction, the worst is over.

This chapter lists common signs of dysfunctional teamwork and the resulting dysfunctional documents. Subsequent chapters describe the steps your team can take to correct this problem.

Failed collaboration

Collaboration is teamwork. Lack of teamwork often results from writer isolation. If writers are isolated from each other, they cannot work coherently on collaborative projects.

Signs of failed collaboration:

- **Team fragmentation**
  Teams split into product groups that have little or nothing to do with one another can become fragmented.

- **Writer isolation**
  Writers working in isolation tend to develop subjective styles and standards for writing and formatting documents.

- **Document "ownership"**
  "Ownership" undermines teamwork by telling individuals they are the ultimate authority for "their" documents.

Failed oversight

Oversight is quality control. It is almost impossible to control the quality of documents without a proactive editing process.

Signs of failed oversight:

- **Missing editors**
  Teams that do not assign editors to systematically evaluate the quality of their documents have no mechanism for diagnosing and treating acute and chronic problems.

- **Junior editors**
  Newly hired writers employed as "junior editors" lack the training, experience, and political influence to provide serious document diagnoses.

- **Peer reviews alone**
  Unless writers have been trained as editors, their peer reviews of each other's writing—as opposed to the content of each other's documents—will tend to be subjective.

- **Copy edits alone**
  Traditional copy edits catch acute symptoms of dysfunction in isolated documents, but they treat symptoms instead of causes. As a result, acute problems can become chronic.

Failed guidelines

Writing guidelines are team agreements. It is almost impossible to reach team agreements about documentation—let alone enforce those agreements—without a formal style guide.

Signs of failed guidelines:

- **Missing guidelines**
  Without writing guidelines that formally record agreements between writing and editing teams, writers develop documents that are out of alignment with each another.

- **Top-down guidelines**
  Imposing one-size-fits-all writing guidelines from "above" the day-to-day work of writers and editors burdens them with third-party "solutions" that do not fit local problems.

- **Unchanging guidelines**
  Writing guidelines need to keep pace with the learning curves of the teams they serve. If they do not, the collective memory of the teams will fragment.

Learning from failure

If you see danger signs of failed collaboration, oversight, or guidelines in your team, it is likely that these problems are reflected in your documentation. The following chapters describe the specific steps your team can take to treat this dysfunction, one document at time.

Dysfunctional Documents

Step 1
Acknowledge problems

Roles	Responsibilities
Writers	Submit worst in-house documents to editors
Editors	Evaluate documents submitted by writers
Managers	Encourage writers to identify problems

The first step in recovery is to acknowledge problems in your documentation. You identify acute problems in individual documents as well as chronic problems in document sets.

Identify acute problems

Most technical writing and editing teams are painfully aware of acute problems in their documentation:

- **Legacy problems**
  Most teams have at least one problem document, typically written by someone who no longer works for the company. Over the years, many different writers have updated parts of the document without touching the whole. At this point, the document looks and feels like a large house constructed without a central building plan.

- **Merger problems**
  If a company merges with another company, it may inherit documentation from the other company. Most likely, this documentation is written and formatted differently. It looks and feels like it comes from another company.

- **Outsourcing problems**
  If your company outsources some documentation projects, you may be confronted with documents that look and feel foreign. If the projects are outsourced to teams whose first language is not English, the documents may not follow basic rules of English language and punctuation, let alone your company or team's writing guidelines.

- **New problems**
  Many teams have at least one new publishing project that presents extraordinary challenges. For example, the project may introduce a new documentation process, such as single sourcing, that raises new issues, such as how to develop content modules that can be assembled into multiple documents in multiple media.

Documents with acute problems are friends in disguise. They present you with glaring problems that are relatively easy to solve precisely because they are obvious. Equally important, they demonstrate that doing nothing is not an option. As a result, your team can start solving problems immediately.

Identify chronic problems

Acute problems in individual documents can alert writing and editing teams to chronic problems in document sets:

- **Multiple authors**
  If documents are written and updated by more than one author, they often reflect the diverse styles of the various authors. For example, inconsistent heading syntax, topic structure, and writing style may be evident.

- **Deep hierarchies**
  If documents have deep hierarchies, they bury information below the surface, where it is difficult for users to find. Often, such complex documents are based on system specifications, which order system features and functions into logical hierarchies. These complex hierarchies help developers but not users who are trying to *do* something. They are centered on the systems, not their use.

- **Unpredictable structures**
  If document structures are not consistent and predictable, they confuse users, who intuitively look for patterns to navigate documents. For example, inconsistent heading syntax sets linguistic patterns and then breaks them. This is like an airport or train station with poor signage.

- **Linear narratives**

  If documents have linear narratives, they force users to read topics in a particular order, like a novel, rather than letting them find answers to specific questions quickly. Linear documents often mix conceptual, procedural, and reference topics in thematic narratives that make users think (learn something) when they want to act (do something). To save time, users may simply ignore the documents altogether.

Although chronic problems can be daunting, they are not qualitatively different from acute problems. In both cases, editors need to identify and illustrate specific problems and solutions in a way that enables the larger team to learn from its mistakes. This process is described in Steps 2–12.

Step 2
Define edit types

Roles	Responsibilities
Writers	Review edit types defined by editors
Editors	Define edit types for writers
Managers	Give editors time to define edit types

The best way to fix acute and chronic problems in documents is through systematic edits that describe and illustrate specific problems and solutions. The best way to assure such systematic edits is to define edit types. The best way to define edit types is to go to the source, *The Levels of* Edit, which compiles edit types into edit levels, or editing service packages. Editors can customize this flexible structure to meet the team's needs.

TIP: The Levels of Edit, *a copyright-free booklet originally published in 1976, can be difficult to find in print. The second edition, which was published in 1980 by the Society for Technical Communication [1], is posted online for easy reference (www.levels-of-edit.com).*

Classic edit types

The Levels of Edit defines nine edit types:

- **Coordination**
  Planning (for example, scheduling) the edit. The seemingly mundane tasks that make up this often-forgotten edit type can eat up a lot of time and should be taken seriously.

- **Policy**
  Making sure the document reflects company policies
  (for example, for copyrights and trademarks).

- **Integrity**
  Making sure the document parts match (for example, table
  of contents, cross-references, and index entries).

- **Screening**
  Making sure the writing meets basic standards (for example,
  for spelling). Sometimes called an "embarrassment edit."

- **Copy Clarification**
  Making sure text and graphics are legible (for example,
  hyphenation, figure callouts, and mathematical formulas).

- **Format**
  Making sure the document uses templates correctly (for
  example, page, paragraph, and character styles).

- **Mechanical Style**
  Making sure the document follows writing guidelines (for
  example, for abbreviations and capitalization).

- **Language**
  Making sure the document is written well (for example, has
  clear headings, concise sentences, and parallel list items).

- **Substantive**
  Making sure content is accurate, complete, and up to date
  (for example, procedure steps describe user tasks correctly).

These edit types provide a flexible structure editors can modify
to meet the team's needs. The editors can group the edit types
into edit levels, as described in Step 3, "Define edit levels."

Stand-alone edit types

The structure of stand-alone documents, such as user manuals, may make it sensible to customize the classic edit types.

For example, some teams remove the following edit types:

- **Coordination**
  Planning is often taken for granted. Some teams do not consider Coordination a legitimate edit type.

- **Integrity**
  Making sure document parts match is not an issue for some teams because their authoring tools "ensure" matching parts.

- **Copy Clarification**
  Making sure text and graphics are legible is not an issue for some teams because their authoring tools "ensure" legible text and graphics.

CAUTION: Coordination, Integrity, and Copy Clarification should not be dismissed casually. Removing Coordination does not remove the associated tasks. As any freelancer can tell you, planning takes time. Not budgeting this time simply hides the costs. Likewise, Integrity and Copy Clarification may be "ensured" by authoring tools, but these tools are only as good as the people who develop them. People, not tools, are the ultimate judges of legibility and integrity.

Some teams add the following edit type:

- **Usability**
  Making sure the document is user-friendly (for example, has a flat structure, meaningful headings, focused topics, and concise procedures).

After editors customize the edit types, they can group them into edit levels, as described in "Stand-alone edit levels" on page 16.

Modular edit types

The structure of documents assembled from a single source (for example, shared modular topics stored in a database and assembled into individual documents) might require editors to seriously rethink edit types.

For example, editors might replace Coordination, Integrity, and Copy Clarification with the following edit types:

- **Label**
  Making sure labels (for example, headings and captions) use a consistent, predictable syntax that indicates module type.

- **Module**
  Making sure modules (for example, topics) answer specific questions: who, what when, where, why, or how.

- **Assembly**
  Making sure modules are organized logically by alphabet, audience, detail, importance, location, sequence, or type.

- **Link**

  Making sure modules are linked (for example, table of contents, cross-references, hyperlinks, and index entries).

- **Usability**

  Making sure assembled documents are usable (for example, each topic and procedure tells a meaningful story).

- **Re-usability**

  Making sure modules are re-usable in any context (for example, modules are easy to read in print and online).

After editors customize the edit types, they can group them into edit levels, as described in "Modular edit levels" on page 17.

Dysfunctional Documents

Step 3
Define edit levels

Roles	Responsibilities
Writers	Review edit levels defined by editors
Editors	Define edit levels for writers
Managers	Give editors time to define edit levels

After editors define edit types, they can group them into edit levels, or service packages, which can be turned into service requests, as described in Appendix B, "Edit request forms."

Classic edit levels

The Levels of Edit defines five edit levels, as shown in Table 1. These edit levels are based on the nine edit types described in "Classic edit types" on page 9.

Table 1 Classic edit levels

Type of edit	Level of edit				
	1	2	3	4	5
Coordination	✓	✓	✓	✓	✓
Policy	✓	✓	✓	✓	✓
Integrity	✓	✓	✓	✓	
Screening	✓	✓	✓	✓	
Copy Clarification	✓	✓	✓		
Format	✓	✓	✓		
Mechanical Style	✓	✓			
Language	✓	✓			
Substantive	✓				

Stand-alone edit levels

For stand-alone documents, editors might group edit types into three edit levels—Technical Edit, Copy Edit, and Proof—as shown in Table 2. The rows highlighted in gray are the edit types they may have removed (-) or added (+) in "Stand-alone edit types" on page 11.

Table 2   Stand-alone edit levels

Type of edit	Level of edit		
	Technical	Copy	Proof
Coordination (-)	✓	✓	✓
Policy	✓	✓	✓
Integrity (-)	✓	✓	✓
Screening	✓	✓	✓
Copy Clarification (-)	✓	✓	✓
Format	✓	✓	✓
Mechanical Style	✓	✓	
Language	✓	✓	
Substantive	✓		
Usability (+)	✓		

Modular edit levels

For single-source documents, editors might group edit types into two levels—Input Edit and Output Edit—as shown in Table 3. Input Edits would examine only source files (for example, topic files in a content management system). Output Edits would examine only output files (for example, database topics assembled into user guides and online help). The rows highlighted in gray are the edit types editors may have removed (-) or added (+) in "Modular edit types" on page 12.

Table 3. Modular edit levels

	Level of edit	
Type of edit	Input	Output
Policy	✓	
Screening	✓	
Mechanical Style	✓	
Language	✓	
Label	✓	
Module	✓	
Coordination (-)	✓	✓
Integrity (-)	✓	✓
Copy Clarification (-)	✓	✓
Assembly		✓
Link		✓
Format		✓
Substantive		✓
Usability (+)		✓
Re-usability (+)		✓

Dysfunctional Documents

Step 4
Edit documents

Roles	Responsibilities
Writers	Do not work on documents while in edit
Editors	Identify global and specific problems in documents
Managers	Encourage honest but diplomatic edits

When reviewing documents, editors should identify problems by type, distinguishing between global and specific problems. Whenever possible, they should cite writing guidelines, as described in Step 10, "Enforce guidelines."

TIP: *Beginning editorial comments with words like "suggest" or "consider" softens the blows, increasing acceptance by writers. They telegraph the editor's wish to start a serious conversation with the writer rather than to dictate terms. These constructive conversations are where synergy between writers and editors often begins.*

Identify problems by type

When editing a document, editors should look for one type of problem at a time, making a separate sweep for each edit type. Unlike the buckshot approach of looking for all problems at once, looking for problems by type enables editors to spot chronic problems quickly. Such a disciplined approach also enables multiple editors to share work on the same document, with each editor looking for distinct types of problems. Most importantly, it reduces the risk of subjective editing. Editors are forced to look for exactly the kinds of problems writers ask them to check (or at least agree to let them check). Such a business agreement defines quantifiable editing services.

TIP: *To avoid confusion, types and levels of edit can be formally requested by writers, using edit request forms. For guidelines and examples of such forms, see Appendix B, "Edit request forms."*

Identify global problems

When editing a document, editors should identify global problems only once:

- **Multiple occurrences**
  If a problem occurs more than once in a document, editors should mark it only once in that document. For example, if a document uses the incorrect abbreviation for a product, page after page, chapter after chapter, it makes no sense to annoy writers by marking every instance of the problem, in effect bleeding red ink all over their document.

- **Patterns**
  If a problem forms a pattern, editors should note the pattern only once in the document and then elaborate in a separate document, as described in Step 5, "Write edit reports." For example, it does not make sense to mark each instance of inconsistent heading syntax because the pattern can be seen only when the headings are listed together. The best way to show the pattern is to compare multiple headings in a separate document (for example, in a table).

By identifying global problems only once in a document, editors avoid overwhelming writers with duplicate comments.

Equally important, they can suggest global solutions in an edit report, as described in "Suggest global solutions" on page 24.

Identify specific problems

Editors should distinguish between problems that occur only once in a document and problems that occur in only one part of that document:

- **Single occurrences in document**
  If a problem occurs only once in a document, editors should mark the problem in the document itself. For example, they can mark misspellings, typos, and other mistakes in a print document with traditional proofreading marks.

  TIP: Proofreading marks are illustrated in standard style guides, such as The Chicago Manual of Style *[2], which includes free online help tools (www.chicagomanualofstyle.org/help-tools).*

- **Single parts of document**
  If a problem occurs in only one part of a document, editors should identify it only once in that part of the document and then elaborate in a separate document, as described in Step 5, "Write edit reports." For example, they can note problems with index entries as they occur and then propose solutions, with negative and positive examples, as described in "Suggest specific solutions" on page 26. In their reports, editors should label comments about single sections with document part titles (for example, "Table of contents," "Chapter 3," or "Index") and page ranges, as needed.

Step 5
Write edit reports

Roles	Responsibilities
Writers	Do not work on documents while in edit
Editors	Write constructive reports about documents
Managers	Give editors time to write detailed reports

Edit reports (sometimes called "comment sheets") accompany document edits. In both print and electronic documents, there is normally not enough space for detailed comments, let alone negative and positive examples. Edit reports make it possible for editors to point out acute or chronic problems and provide detailed suggestions for major changes, such as relabeling topics, restructuring procedures, and so on.

In edit reports, is helpful for editors to separate global problems found throughout the document from specific problems found only in individual sections of the document. Each item in the report should be illustrated with negative and positive examples, as shown in Appendix C, "Writing guidelines." Whenever possible, editors should cite writing guidelines, as described in Step 10, "Enforce guidelines."

TIP: Edit reports start detailed conversations with writers about guidelines. Potentially, each entry in an edit report can serve as the basis for a proposed entry to a style guide. For details, see Step 7, "Propose guidelines."

Suggest global solutions

Editors should begin their edit reports by identifying global
problems found throughout the document and by suggesting
global solutions, such as the following:

- **Policy**
  Provide up-to-date product names, terminology lists,
  and so on.

- **Integrity**
  Suggest consistent heading syntax, topic structure,
  procedure structure, index entry syntax, and so on.

- **Screening**
  List corrections to global problems with grammar,
  punctuation, spelling, and so on.

- **Format**
  Show how to correct formatting problems with cross-
  references, figures, headers, footers, lists, steps, tables,
  typefaces, and so on.

- **Mechanical Style**
  Show how to follow style guidelines for abbreviations,
  capitalization, hyphenation, and so on.

- **Language**
  Show how to improve writing style with active voice,
  conciseness, parallel construction, present tense, second
  person, and so on.

- **Substantive**

  Correct technical inaccuracies (for example, incorrect version numbers) found throughout the document.

  TIP: If substantive problems are found only in specific sections, they should be included in another part of the edit report, as described in "Suggest specific solutions" on page 26.

- **Usability**

  Show how to improve the usability of the document (for example, by restructuring poorly constructed lists, paragraphs, procedures, and so on).

The global problem categories in this list are based on the edit types described in Step 2, "Define edit types."

CAUTION: Edit types are not ideal categories for global comments in edit reports. A more writer-friendly approach is to list these comments alphabetically by keyword. For example, under the section "Global comments," an editor might include the subsections "Abbreviations," "Capitalization," "Person," "Tense," "Voice," and so on. That way, writers can see the big-ticket issues at a glance. For an illustration of this approach, see Appendix C, "Writing guidelines."

Suggest specific solutions

Editors should conclude their reports with specific solutions to specific problems found in specific sections of the document, such as the following:

- **Front matter**
  Point out policy violations (for example, incorrect copyright symbols) in the title page, copyright page, trademark list, prefaces, and so on.

- **Chapters and appendices**
  Suggest solutions to substantive or stylistic problems (for example, inaccurate procedure steps) found only in isolated chapters or appendices.

- **Glossary**
  Suggest solutions to substantive or stylistic problems (for example, with abbreviations, parallel construction, person, tense, and voice) in glossary terms and definitions.

- **Index**
  Suggest consistent index entry syntax for different topic types (for example, conceptual, procedural, and reference topics). Also point out substantive imbalances (for example, entries for some document sections but not others).

An edit report is an expansion of comments added by the editor to the writer's document. In inline comments, editors should reference relevant sections of the edit report (for example, by heading). In edit reports, they should reference inline comments (for example, by page number).

Step 6
Evaluate edit reports

Roles	Responsibilities
Writers	Evaluate edit reports honestly and fairly
Editors	Submit edit reports to writers for evaluation
Managers	Meditate disputes between writers and editors

Just as writers use edit requests to schedule document edits, they use edit reports to evaluate the quality of those edits.

Evaluate all suggestions

Before implementing suggestions in edit reports, writers should evaluate them carefully:

- **Existing guidelines (mandatory)**
  If suggestions explicitly reference existing style guidelines, the suggestions are all but mandatory. For example, if the company or team style guide prohibits passive voice, and the edit report suggests ways to avoid passive voice, writers should attempt to follow the suggestion.

- **Potential guidelines (optional)**
  If suggestions do not explicitly reference existing style guidelines, the suggestions are optional. For example, if the company or team style guide does not mention active or passive voice, but an edit report suggests using active voice

wherever possible, writers should consider implementing the suggestion, as time permits.

TIP: *If writers like a suggestion well enough to implement it, they should consider proposing the suggestion as a potential guideline to the larger team, as described in Step 7, "Propose guidelines."*

- **Personal preferences (prohibited)**
  If suggestions simply reflect the personal preferences of a particular editor, writers can—and should—ignore them. For example, if the company or team style guide does not mention boldface, but an edit report asserts, without supporting argument, that boldface should be used for all items that appear in a user interface, writers should talk to the editor or even their own manager. Editors who assert their own personal preferences without objective justification do more harm than good.

Implement good suggestions

Before implementing suggestions from editors, writers should do the following:

- **Ask questions**
  Writers almost always have questions and comments about edit reports. For example, they may not understand a suggested way of restructuring their procedures. Without clarification, they cannot implement the suggestion. Likewise, they may completely disagree with a style guideline. In both cases, a meeting between the writer and editor can help resolve disagreements before they turn into entrenched fights between writing and editing teams.

> **TIP:** *Disagreements are inevitable and sometimes desirable. Resolving them in a constructive manner can help establish a productive working relationship between writers and editors.*

- **Prioritize suggestions**
  After writers decide which suggestions they want to implement, they should prioritize them. Writers should implement suggestions that support existing guidelines first. If time permits, they can then implement the other suggestions. If not, they can wait until the next edit cycle.

Identify best practices

After writers implement suggestions, they should hold a so-called *post mortem* with editors to discuss the following:

- **Worst practices**
  If writers and editors sit down together and honestly evaluate what went wrong in an edit, they can take steps to improve the process. For example, if they did not allocate enough time for the current edit cycle, they may want to reduce the number of edit types in the next edit cycle.

- **Best practices**
  The closer together writers and editors work, the more likely they are to have breakthroughs that they can share with their teams. For example, while implementing a suggestion in an edit report, a writer may radically simplify the structure of a document in a way that is extremely popular with users. With the help of the editor, the writer can then propose this breakthrough as a new guideline, as described in Step 7, "Propose guidelines."

Step 7
Propose guidelines

Roles	Responsibilities
Writers	Help editors pick best practices from recent edits
Editors	Compile best practices into proposed guidelines
Managers	Encourage writers and editors to propose guidelines

After writers and editors identify best practices, based on individual document edits, editors compile them into formal guideline proposals, which they present to managers.

Compile proposals

When compiling best practices into proposed guidelines, editors should be careful to avoid misunderstandings:

- **Avoid redundancy**
  Editors should make sure that the proposed guidelines are not already included in the existing company or team style guide. Likewise, they should combine duplicate best practices taken from various edits into single proposals, using real examples from as many edits as possible.

- **Give credit to writers**
  When presenting best practices to writing managers, editors should always give credit where credit is due, identifying specific proposals with the writers who co-developed them.

Crediting writers also helps avoid the impression that editors are imposing their own preferences on the team.

- **List pros and cons**
  Editors should make it easy for managers to see the results of proposals by designing each proposal as a potential style guide entry. They should include arguments for and against each proposal, presenting as much information as possible to make an intelligent decision.

Distribute proposals

Editors should distribute proposals to all managers who are authorized to make style guide decisions:

- **Writing managers**
  Managers of all writing groups that use the style guide

- **Managing editors**
  Managers of all editing groups that support the style guide

TIP: For best results, editors should distribute proposals in easy-to-print formats at least two weeks before meeting with managers. They should also make deadlines explicit. Firmness and formality are more helpful in the distribution process than overly casual "friendliness." This is a business transaction and should be treated as such.

Step 8
Evaluate guidelines

Roles	Responsibilities
Writers	Present own guideline proposals to own manager
Editors	Present all guideline proposals to all managers
Managers	Establish review process and vote on all proposals

Guideline proposals should be presented to writing managers and managing editors. For example, if your organization has four writing teams, each associated with a given product team, as well as one centralized editing team, voting managers would include four writing managers and one managing editor.

CAUTION: Although it is sometimes useful to have key writers help present proposals for which they have particular expertise, it is important that these writers, like the editors present, have no voting rights. They are simply "expert witnesses." Managers, not writing and editing experts, have the final say in what is ultimately a political process. Without explicit management support, quality control has no mandate. This mandate is critical to Step 10, "Enforce guidelines."

Establish a review process

Before voting on guideline proposals, managers need to establish a review process:

- **Quorum**
  No vote can take place without all voting managers present. Managers can appear physically or virtually (for example, via video conference).

- **Substitution**
  Although voting managers who cannot attend the approval meeting can appoint substitutes (for example, lead writers), holding meeting with all voting managers present helps ensure that votes are respected and enforced.

- **Unanimity**
  To ensure unconditional management support of all guidelines, each proposal requires unanimous approval by voting managers. Unanimous decisions counterbalance natural competition between teams, forcing managers to compromise to get the guidelines they care about most.

  TIP: Consensus is not an accident. Once managers understand the rules, they engage in "horse trading." It is wise for editors to coordinate (stage) trades privately, ahead of the formal review.

- **Modification**
  Before approving proposals, managers may modify them. For example, managers may fine-tune glossary terminology guidelines, based on new corporate branding guidelines.

By approving proposed guidelines, managers agree to enforce them within their own teams.

Review individual proposals

When presenting proposed guidelines to managers for review, editors should do the following:

- **Propose guidelines**
  Walk managers through the written proposal for each guideline. Present arguments for and against each proposal, as well as any relevant history. Often, the most compelling argument is real experience in the field. It is extremely helpful to describe this experience in detail and answer all questions, no matter how trivial they may seem.

  CAUTION: How proposals are presented to managers can make or break the credibility of editors. Editors should be careful to stay in character as honest brokers in the proposal process. In effect, editors present themselves as messengers, not proposers.

- **Coordinate voting**
  Reiterate the rules for voting to managers. Proposals should be approved by unanimous vote only. If all managers are on record as having approved a proposed guideline, they will support its enforcement.

- **Record results**
  Serve as meeting scribes. Editors should record the results of each vote on each proposal, as well as any pertinent corrections from managers. After the proposal review meeting, they should send meeting minutes to all voting managers, so everything is recorded in writing.

Verify proposal decisions

To verify the decisions made by managers in the proposal review meeting, editors should do the following:

- **Compile**
  Compile all approved proposals into a new document that describes and illustrates the guidelines exactly as they will appear in the style guide (including any modifications made by managers during the approval process).

- **Summarize**
  Summarize the new guidelines that were approved by managers in a memo addressed to those managers.

- **Distribute**
  Send the memo and preliminary guidelines to managers for final written approval. If managers do not respond to the memo, they tacitly approve of all preliminary guidelines.

  TIP: Give managers a hard deadline (for example, two weeks) to object to any new guideline. Make it clear that non-response from any manager will be counted as approval by that manager of all proposed guidelines. This seemingly draconian step prevents future "misunderstandings" with the very managers needed to support the new guidelines when the going gets tough.

- **Modify**
  If any manager objects to any guideline, attempt to correct the guideline. If that is not possible, remove the guideline from the list of approved guidelines and add it to the list of proposals for the next review meeting (for example, in the next quarter or year).

Dysfunctional Documents

Step 8
Evaluate guidelines

This verification process serves three purposes. First, it prevents interdepartmental misunderstandings, which can quickly escalate into turf wars. Second, it enables managers to make sure that the guidelines they voted for are the guidelines they get. Finally, it provides editors with tangible evidence of management buy-in for guidelines they will have to enforce.

Step 9
Publish guidelines

Roles	Responsibilities
Writers	Review updates to style guide
Editors	Compile and distribute updated style guide
Managers	Verify updates to style guide

After new guidelines are approved, editors need to integrate them into the existing company or team style guide and then distribute that to all affected writers, editors, and managers.

TIP: If your company or team does not already have a style guide, the newly approved guidelines should be formatted as a style guide, with the appropriate title page, revisions page, and so on. Guidelines subsequently approved by managers (for example, in quarterly or annual reviews) should then be added to this guide, with the updates carefully noted and dated on the revisions page.

Compile approved guidelines

To compile the newly approved guidelines, editors should do the following:

- **Add**
  Add the newly approved guidelines to the style guide. If the style guide has a simple structure (for example, guidelines are ordered alphabetically), adding new guidelines is easy. If the style guide has a complex structure (for example,

guidelines are ordered thematically), adding new guidelines can be less straightforward.

- **Synchronize**
Verify that the newly approved guidelines do not duplicate or contradict existing guidelines. Although editors should compare new guidelines with the existing style guide before proposing them, it is wise to double-check newly approved guidelines before adding them to the style guide. If editors find duplications or contradictions, they should alert approving managers and propose a solution (for example, removing an old guideline that contradicts a new guideline).

CAUTION: It is not uncommon for guidelines to have unintended consequences. For example, a new guideline for boldface usage may indirectly contradict old guidelines for writing procedure steps that contain clickable interface items. Before updating the style guide, editors should look carefully for potential contradictions.

- **Date**
Include the release date of the new style guide. Editors can then cite the release date when citing guidelines in future edits. Writers can do the same when rejecting specific edits.

- **Back up**
Archive each version of the style guide for future reference. Style guides serve as the collective memory for writing and editing teams. Over time, these teams tend to change their collective minds. If editors archive each version of the style guide, they make it easier for teams to remember the sometimes twisted history of past decisions.

TIP: *Archives help build fault tolerance into the style guide by recording the history of team decisions. This record enables teams to learn from their mistakes systematically. Editors can aid this process by explicitly noting reversals of former guidelines.*

- **Proofread**
  Read through the style guide very carefully, looking for *anything* that might lead to conflict. Like a legal text, the style guide will be examined closely by those who enforce it as well as those whose documents are enforced in its name.

- **Summarize**
  Summarize updates in the style guide (for example, in a specially designated revisions section). In addition, summarize the updates in a cover memo. Address the memo to everyone who will be affected by the changes: managers, writers, editors, translators, and so on.

Distribute approved guidelines

As a rule, it is best for editors to distribute updated guidelines electronically:

- **Central storage**
  The easiest way to distribute updated guidelines is to post each version of the style guide electronically in a central location (for example, on an intranet or in a document management system). Centralized storage enables any team member to find the latest style guide from any location. It also avoids inherent problems with email (for example, file attachment size limits).

TIP: *If possible, create a permanent hyperlink to the style guide, so team members only have to bookmark it once. Most document management systems support permanent universal resource locators (URLs) and so-called "tiny URLs."*

- **Email alert**
Send an email alert to all style guide recipients that summarizes the cover memo. Make sure to send the alert from an email address specially designated for the style guide. This email address will become the *de facto* target for comments and complaints about the style guide.

TIP: *Creating a special email address associated with a "style guide editor" role, rather than with individual editors, depersonalizes the process, making it clear to everyone that the person managing the style guide is simply a messenger for team decisions, not someone dictating personal preferences to the team. A role-based address also makes it possible for more than one editor to address questions, comments, and complaints.*

- **Feedback loop**
Ask recipients of the style guide for feedback. Although updates result from a formal proposal review process, distribution itself can attract valuable feedback from surprising sources. Some team members invariably treat style guide releases as an opportunity to find problems, however miniscule, with updates. Harness this reflex.

Editors should distribute the style guide to anyone who will be affected by it. In addition to the core writing and editing teams, recipients can include offsite writers, editors, graphic designers, translators, usability testers, and consultants.

Step 10
Enforce guidelines

Roles	Responsibilities
Writers	Follow approved writing guidelines
Editors	Cite approved writing guidelines in edits
Managers	Support guideline enforcement in edits

Writing guidelines and editorial enforcement have a symbiotic relationship. Enforcement without guidelines is arbitrary, and guidelines without enforcement are toothless. When properly coordinated, however, guideline development and enforcement systematically improve the quality of the team's writing.

The best way to enforce writing guidelines is for editors to cite specific passages from the style guide, chapter and verse, in *every* comment of *every* edit. The goal is to make it easy for writers to do the right thing. The more editors (service providers) sweat, the less writers (customers) have to.

Cite guidelines in edits

Every comment in every edit should cite a specific guideline in the style guide, as described in the following steps:

- Step 4, "Edit documents"
- Step 5, "Write edit reports"

Writers are focused on information development, not writing guidelines. Their quarterly objectives and annual evaluations are based on writing, not editing. In edit reports, editors should gently remind writers of agreed-upon guidelines by quoting the pertinent section of the style guide by topic title and page number. Such detailed citations highlight the sections of the style guide that most affect particular writers and their documents. In effect, they are customized style guides.

TIP: *Over time, editors can compile such quotations into short lists of common style problems. Such lists can help writing teams learn new guidelines without (re)reading the style guide cover to cover. They can also be re-used by editors in subsequent edits.*

When editors cite agree-upon style guidelines in edits, they also prevent their own personal preferences from creeping in. By enforcing guidelines they may personally disagree with, editors demonstrate their objectivity and help build team trust.

Demonstrate guidelines

Editors can make it easier for writers to understand complex guidelines by providing detailed negative and positive examples in edit reports. For example, if editors find chronic problems in procedure steps within a document set, they can describe and demonstrate the problems in detail, and then describe and demonstrate proposed solutions as positive counter-examples.

Editors can use detailed examples to do the following:

- **Initiate conversations**
  Initiate conversations with writers about complex guidelines (for example, heading syntax or procedure structure).

Dysfunctional Documents

- **Suggest changes**

  Suggest major changes to documents without damaging the content itself. In effect, detailed suggestions are electronic white boards to walk through new ideas.

- **Suggest guidelines**

  Suggest new guidelines to the team. Examples enable editors to demonstrate how a given guideline will be implemented.

TIP: *Editors can make it even easier for writers to implement simple guidelines by automating them. For details, see Step 12, "Automate guidelines."*

Dysfunctional Documents

Step 11
Update guidelines

Roles	Responsibilities
Writers	Implement good guidelines, appeal bad guidelines
Editors	Establish process for making exceptions
Managers	Appoint ombudspersons to mediate disputes

Although writing guidelines are approved by managers, they are tested by reality. If the guidelines are not realistic, writers will let managers and editors know. Editors can then alert the rest of the team in the next style guide review cycle.

Implement practical guidelines

Good guidelines work well in practice. These guidelines are easy to understand, remember, and implement. For example, a simple heading syntax guideline may tell writers to begin procedure headings with verbs and to begin non-procedure headings with nouns.

TIP: Simple guidelines also make it easy to develop related guidelines. For example, guidelines for consistent heading syntax for specific topic types makes it easy to develop corollary guidelines for index entries. If implemented correctly, such guidelines can even be automated. For details, see Step 12, "Automate guidelines".

If guidelines work well in practice, writers should implement them. If writers have difficulty implementing guidelines, they should seek out the help of editors. For details, see "Demonstrate guidelines" on page 44.

Appeal or revise impractical guidelines

Bad guidelines are those that do not work well in practice. These guidelines are difficult to understand, remember, and implement. For example, writers may try to follow a guideline that forbids the use of Latin abbreviations, only to find out that Latin abbreviations are preferred by their target audience (for example, doctors or scientists). If guidelines do not work well in practice, writers and editors should appeal or revise them (for example, indicating when they apply and when not).

Propose new guidelines

As writers implement guidelines in real documents, they can determine which guidelines work in practice and which do not. With the heightened sensitivity that comes from focusing on guideline implementation, they can more easily spot problems in their documents that are not addressed by the existing guidelines. Writers should immediately note any problems, complete with examples, and then contact editors.

Editors can help writers to transform this raw information into tentative solutions, which can then be immediately tested by the writers. This back and forth between theory and practice can be used to develop best practices, which eventually become the basis for future guideline proposals.

Add new guidelines

Writers or editors may be so enthusiastic about a suggestion that worked well in a particular document that they want to propose it to the entire team as a guideline. For example, if writers and editors streamline procedure steps in online help in a way that is popular with users, they may want to propose this usability innovation for inclusion in the style guide.

Change existing guidelines

Even if writers whole-heartedly agree with an existing guideline, they sometimes run into practical problems when trying to implement it. For example, writers may agree with the guideline "always use active voice" because, in their experience, active voice is often clearer than passive voice. Then, when developing troubleshooting topics, they may discover that the clarity of active voice has the unintended consequence of implying that users are responsible for the problems they are troubleshooting. In this case, writers and editors may want to include an exception to the guideline.

When writers and editors discover an exception to an existing guideline, they should write it down so they can later propose its addition to the style guide. Exceptions help writers follow otherwise valid guidelines.

Establish guideline exceptions

Managers and editors should establish a process for handling exceptions to style guide rules:

- **Guideline owners**
  Managers should select ombudspersons (for example, some combination of writing managers, managing editors, lead writers, and senior editors) to serve as guideline owners between review cycles. These individuals decide whether to issue temporary exceptions to the guidelines.

- **Feedback process**
  Editors should establish a formal process for making exceptions to guidelines. This process should include documentation of the exceptions. A good place to put such information is in the style guide itself, with exceptions treated as guideline updates.

Exceptions enable teams to circumvent harmful rules without violating team decisions. They also serve as an early warning system for bad guidelines.

Step 12
Automate guidelines

Roles	Responsibilities
Writers	Help develop tools, if appropriate
Editors	Coordinate automation with tool specialists
Managers	Support the automation process, as needed

One extremely effective way to implement (some) writing guidelines is to automate them by building them right into publishing tools (for example, a content management system).

Because editors coordinate guideline development, they are the ideal team members to coordinate guideline automation. However, unless editors are exceptionally technical, they will need the help of tool specialists.

TIP: *Editors should actively build relationships with tool experts for just such moments. These experts can be IT developers with a special interest in publishing or the one person in a writing team who likes to "wrestle" with the publishing "beast" in the "basement."*

Identify solutions for automation

Before editors automate guidelines, they need to identify specific problems and solutions:

1 **Problems**

List the most frequently violated guidelines. Use edit reports to identify and rank the violations. Explicitly cite the guidelines being violated.

2 **Solutions**

For each listed violation, specify potential automation techniques. For example, to encourage the use of active voice, editors might indicate ways in which the grammar checker in the team's content management system could be modified. As a more complex example, editors might set up a table that pairs guidelines for topic heading syntax with guidelines for index entry syntax, making it easy for tool developers to understand the team's goal of generating index entries automatically, based on heading syntax.

Approve automation solutions

After identifying solutions for automation, editors need to request permission from all affected teams (for example, writing, editing, translation, and IT groups). The process is similar to that described in Step 7, "Propose guidelines."

For each automation request, editors should follow a formal approval process:

1 **Propose**

Formally present automation proposals to the managers of all affected groups. At a minimum, each proposal should list the pros and cons of automating a given guideline.

TIP: Although editors and tool experts should never automate guidelines without the explicit approval of affected teams, they need to do their homework before proposing an automation solution to those teams. Often, this will involve setting up a small prototype that demonstrates the viability of the solution.

2 **Approve**

Request that the managers of all affected teams formally review automation proposals. Given that guidelines are not usually automated regularly (for example, on a quarterly basis), such meetings will most likely be rare. Editors and tool developers can implement an automation solution only if all managers who review it formally authorize its implementation. As with style guidelines, unanimity is critical to the success of automation solutions.

CAUTION: Editors should record all decisions about an automation proposal review in writing. They will need this paper trail if anything goes wrong in the automation.

Set up a cross-functional team

After getting formal approval for an automation solution, editors should set up (and lead) a cross-functional team:

- **Content team**
  Assign writers who will use the automation to test it. These team members are the first users of the automation.

- **Technical team**
  Assign technically savvy writers (for example, template builders), IT experts (for example, programmers with an interest in publications), or both to implement the approved automation. These team members are automation service providers.

Build guidelines into tools

To build a guidelines into a tools, the content and technical teams should follow these steps:

1 **Write specification**
  The content team writes a specification for the automation that describes the final product and explains its use.

2 **Build automation**
  Based on the specification, the technical team builds the automation (for example, automatic indexing based on heading syntax in a content management system).

3 **Implement automation locally**
  The content team implements the automated solution on one sample project in real time to identify any bugs.

4 **Fix automation**
   The technical team fixes any bugs found by the content team in the sample project.

5 **Implement automation globally**
   The technical team rolls out the automation to all other teams. The content team presents the automation to the other teams and gathers feedback for the technical team.

Build boilerplate documents

In addition to automation tools, the cross-functional team can develop so-called "boilerplate" of standard document parts:

- Title page
- Copyright page
- Prefaces
- Chapter TOCs
- Procedure steps
- Glossary entries
- Index entries

Each boilerplate part should demonstrate guidelines, as described in "Demonstrate guidelines" on page 44.

Appendix A
The Levels of Edit

The Levels of Edit is a copyright-free booklet by Robert Van Buren and Mary Fran Buehler that was first published in 1976 at Jet Propulsion Laboratory. A second edition was published in 1980 by the Society for Technical Communication [1].

TIP: *Both editions are difficult to find in print. An electronic copy of the second edition is posted online (www.levels-of-edit.com).*

Figure 1 shows the forward, which says: "the levels-of-edit concept was designed from the beginning to be adaptable to the individual needs of different publications organizations."

Figure 1 *The Levels of Edit*: Foreword

Figure 2 shows two pages from Section II, "The-Levels-of-Edit Concept," explaining how edit types can be compiled into various edit levels, or editing service packages. The table on the right is replicated in Table 1, "Classic edit levels," on page 15 of the current guide. It is also customized in Table 2, "Stand-alone edit levels," on page 16 and in Table 3, "Modular edit levels," on page 17. These customized tables illustrate how the flexible levels-of-edit structure can be used for different purposes.

Figure 2 *The Levels of Edit*: Concept

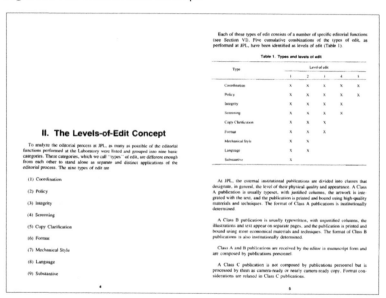

Figure 3 shows two pages from Section VI, "The Types of Edit," which describes each edit type in detail. Editors should use the same amount of detail when defining edit types for their team. The process for doing so is described in Step 2, "Define edit types," of the current guide.

Figure 3 *The Levels of Edit*: Types of edit

symbols, treatment of facsimile copy such as computer printouts, illustration sizing, photograph retouching, and others.

For the most part, these considerations are independent of the context, and so are properly design (format) considerations. Such elements of format, which are not normally of concern to the editor, are not listed here as part of the Format Edit. However, the editor may override any standardized format requirement if this is necessary to convey the meaning properly.

G. Mechanical Style Edit

The Mechanical Style Edit is performed to bring the mechanics of the text and figures into consistent conformity with a specified style. Such mechanical aspects include, for example, capitalization, abbreviations, use of numbers, use of bold face and italics for symbols, and sequencing of reference, figure, and table citations.

For JPL Publications, the basic reference for mechanical style is the *U.S. Government Printing Office Style Manual* (Ref. 2). For other publications (e.g., a journal article or meeting paper), mechanical style will follow whatever guidelines are furnished by the journal, the meeting organizers, or the author.

Where there are no style guidelines, and with the concurrence of the author, the editor may (1) use Ref. 2 or (2) in manuscripts with inconsistent style, standardize on the stylistic choices used in the majority of instances.

The Mechanical Style Edit ensures appropriate and consistent style in the following areas:

(1) Capitalization related to content (as contrasted with all-caps format in headings or figures; e.g., "Earth" vs "earth").

(2) Spelling (e.g., "disk" vs "disc"). Note that correct spelling is specified in the Screening Edit, but there is no requirement in the Screening Edit for consistency between two acceptable forms.

(3) Word compounding (e.g., "non-parallel" vs "nonparallel"), including treatment of hyphens in unit modifiers (e.g., "solid state" vs "solid-state" as unit modifier).

(4) Form (words vs digits) and construction (nouns vs adjectives) of numerals (e.g., level one, level 1, first level).

(5) Form and use of particular symbols, letters, words, or combinations thereof, including acronyms and abbreviations (especially units of mea-

surement). Includes the use of alphanumeric or other symbols in headings, listings, and paragraphs to indicate sequence and/or subordination.

(6) Bibliographic reference style, including sequencing of the elements of each reference (i.e., author, title, etc.).

(7) Use of italics, bold face, script, or other special fonts in content-related distinctive treatment of particular letters, symbols, or words.

(8) Sequential appearance of citations and of the elements cited, such as references, equations, figures, tables, footnotes, and appendixes.

(9) Horizontal spacing between letters, symbols, and words, and around mathematical operators ($+$, $=$, $>$, etc.).

(10) Use of project or organization nomenclature.

(11) Callouts used to identify curves, data points, ordinates, and abscissas on figures.

(12) Presentation of comparable material from slide to slide or viewgraph to viewgraph in a series of visual aids.

H. Language Edit

The Language Edit is an in-depth review concerned with the way in which the ideas in a report are expressed, regardless of the format (e.g., type font) or mechanical style (e.g., capitalization). The Language Edit may be performed separately, without other types of edit. This may happen, for example, in a type of editorial assistance offered when an author wishes to have the language polished in a manuscript before he submits it to his management for approval. The editor returns the edited manuscript to the author, who arranges to have it typed. In this kind of editorial assistance, it is important to remember that the pure Language Edit does not include marking for mechanical style or for format.

All editorial changes in a Language Edit are made on the basis of specific and identifiable reasons rather than the personal preferences of the editor. A Language Edit covers the following areas:

(1) Spelling, according to *Webster's Third New International Dictionary* (Ref. 3), preferably using the first of any two or more acceptable versions.

(2) Grammar and syntax.

(3) Punctuation, according to the *U.S. Government Printing Office Style Manual* (Ref. 2).

(4) Usage, according to the usage level represented by *Modern American Usage* (Ref. 4).

20

21

Appendix B
Edit request forms

To formalize the editing process, editors should develop edit request forms in close collaboration with writers. The forms are templates for binding agreements between writers and editors. They can also be used to train new editors and to track editing progress by document and version. To get a glimpse of what such forms might look like, see "Sample forms" on page 66.

Quantify expectations

The best way to develop an edit request form is to get input from internal customers (writers and writing managers) and their service providers (editors and managing editors).

Editors quantify services

Editors design edit request forms to quantify their services:

- **Services**
  Editors can define which editing services are possible. For example, they might define eight edit types: Coordination, Policy, Screening, Format, Mechanical Style, Language, Substantive, and Usability. They might then group the eight edit types into three edit service levels: Technical Edit, Copy Edit, and Proof, as shown in Figure 4 on page 67.

- **Timeframes**

  Editors can define how long each editing service takes. For example, they might set hourly page counts for three levels of edit service, based on the historical experience that a Technical Edit takes twice as long to complete as a Copy Edit and three times as long to complete as a Proof. The hourly page count for a Technical Edit would then be one-half of that for a Copy Edit and one-third of that for a Proof.

In this way, editors can use edit request forms to quantify the time differences for the services they offer.

Writers quantify requirements

Writers fill out edit request forms to quantify requirements:

- **Needs**

  Writers can define which edit types and levels they need for a given project. For example, they might choose a Technical Edit for a finished document, but specifically exclude the Usability edit type because the document is currently being tested on live users in a usability lab. At the same time, they might ask editors to suggest ways to improve specific graphs with which they are having trouble.

- **Deadlines**

  Writers can define when they want a given edit to begin and end. For example, they might request a Technical Edit of a 200-page document to be completed in five working days. If editing metrics indicate that such an edit would take two weeks, writers would have to make a choice: either decrease the number of edit types or increase the number of days.

In this way, writers can determine which services are possible in a given timeframe.

Managers quantify results

Managers analyze edit request forms to quantify results:

- **Costs**
  Managers can track times for different edit levels. For example, by averaging numbers for a given year, they might see that Technical Edits take three times as long as Proofs and twice as long as Copy Edits. They might also notice that Technical Edits are performed by experienced editors, while Proofs are performed by novice editors. In this way, they could uncover hidden costs.

- **Quality**
  Managers can quantify improvements in documents over time. For example, if a document required a Technical Edit for its first release, a Copy Edit for its second release, and a Proof for its third release, it most likely improved over time. On the other hand, if the document went through three Technical Edits in a row, that might indicate a recurrent problem that had to be solved repeatedly.

Managers can use forms as historical records to quantify quality improvements and the associated costs.

Answer questions

Edit request forms should answer basic questions:

- **Who**
  List the names of the main writer and the main editor assigned to the document. An edit request is a formal contract between these two people.

- **What**
  List the complete title, version, and size (for example, page or topic count) of the document to be edited.

- **When**
  List the start and due dates of the edit, based on metrics established for edit types and levels.

- **Where**
  List the electronic locations of input and output documents, along with the document formats.

- **Why**
  List the desired outcomes of the edit (for example, document reorganization) in a comments section.

- **How**
  List edit levels and types requested as well as the format of the document (for example, Adobe FrameMaker).

Formalize processes

Editors should make sure that edit request forms strictly define edit processes:

- **Design forms for usability**
  When editors design internal edit request forms, they should apply all the usability lessons normally applied to external user documentation. For example, they should design a compact form that fits on one page. They can place detailed descriptions of edit levels, cost metrics, and so on in a separate document.

  TIP: *If the U.S. Government can design a one-page income tax form called "EZ," editors can design a one-page edit request form.*

- **Update forms regularly**
  Editors should enable writers to add extra instructions to edit request forms. For example, some writers may request that editors take a close look at their document organization or index. If many writers make the same additional request, editors may want to add another edit type to make such a request easier to input (for example, through a checkbox).

- **Distribute forms electronically**
  Unless all writers and editors—including contractors—work at one physical location, editors should develop an electronic form (for example, an Adobe Acrobat PDF) that can be distributed, filled out, and submitted online.

- **Archive forms electronically**
  Editors should archive all edit requests electronically so they can be accessed by all team members (for example, on the

company intranet). These forms provide a historical record of edits. As such, they can be used to recalibrate edit metrics (for example, the times and costs for different edit levels). Such archiving makes it much easier for managers to quantify the costs and benefits of edits.

Sample forms

This section includes sample request forms for two edit types:

- **Stand-alone edits**
  The form shown in Figure 4 on page 67 is based on Table 2, "Stand-alone edit levels," on page 16. The form can be used to configure edits for stand-alone user guides and helpsets.

- **Modular edits**
  The form shown in Figure 5 on page 68 is based on Table 3, "Modular edit levels," on page 17. The form can be used to configure edits for single-source modules as well as assembled documents.

The edit levels and types, as well as the applications listed, are examples that illustrate the mechanics of edit reports.

Figure 4 Sample edit request form: Stand-alone documents

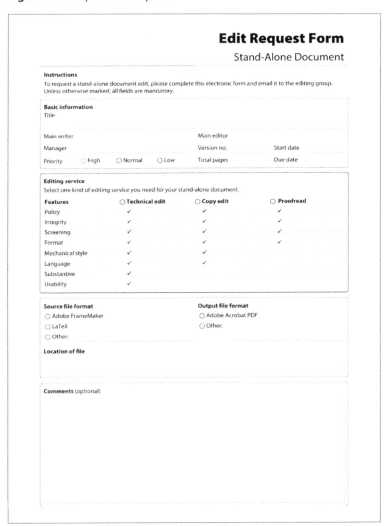

Figure 5 Sample edit request form: Modular documents

Appendix C
Writing guidelines

This appendix contains guidelines taken from style guides at real companies around the world.

TIP: *The guidelines are reproduced from* Single Sourcing: Building Modular Documentation *[3] and* Indexing: A Nuts-and-Bolts Guide for Technical Writers *[4].*

You can follow the structure of the guidelines to build your own style guide from the ground up, based on individual edits. The point is not the specific guidelines listed here but the example-driven approach to developing and illustrating them.

TIP: *Before building a style guide, (re)read* The Elements of Style, *written by William Strunk Jr. in 1918, revised by E. B. White in 1959, and republished in 1988 [5]. This small book is a model of conciseness.*

Abbreviations

Abbreviations are shortened forms of words and phrases. To enable users to easily identify abbreviations anywhere, spell them out the first time they are mentioned in a document. Use common and trademarked abbreviations. Avoid uncommon abbreviations, especially Latin abbreviations.

Common abbreviations

To make common abbreviations understandable, spell them out the first time you mention them in a document. Thereafter, use the abbreviations without spellouts.

First mention	Thereafter
Extensible Markup Language (XML)	XML
Portable Document Format (PDF)	PDF

Latin abbreviations

Latin abbreviations are often unfamiliar to users. Use English equivalents of Latin abbreviations.

Change	To
e.g.	for example,
etc.	and so on

Trademarked abbreviations

Trademarked abbreviations are usually more familiar to users than the words they abbreviate. Use trademarked abbreviations rather than the words they abbreviate.

Change	To
International Business Machines	IBM

Uncommon abbreviations

Avoid abbreviations that are not familiar to users. Spell out uncommon abbreviations wherever they appear.

Change	To
CRC	Cyclical Redundancy Checking
DES	Data Encryption Standard
UMB	upper memory block

Uncommon words

Occasionally, abbreviations are better known to users than their spellouts. In these instances, present the abbreviations with their spellouts in parentheses the first time you mention them in a document. Thereafter, use the abbreviations only.

First mention	Thereafter
TIFF (Tagged Image File Format)	TIFF
GIF (Graphics Interchange Format)	GIF
JPEG (Joint Photographic Experts Group)	JPEG

Capitalization

Consistent capitalization improves document usability. Use consistent capitalization in document titles, section headings, figure and table captions, lists, and glossaries.

Capitalizing document titles

Title capitalization (Abc Def) is standard for document titles. When capitalizing document titles, follow this standard.

Change	To
AcmePro installation guide	*AcmePro Installation Guide*

Capitalizing headings

For headings, use sentence capitalization (Abc def). Title capitalization (Abc Def) makes it difficult for users to recognize proper nouns.

Change	To
Installing an Oracle Database	Installing an Oracle database

Capitalizing captions

For figure and table captions, use sentence capitalization (Abc def), not title capitalization (Abc Def), to make it easier to distinguish proper nouns.

Change	To
Figure 1. Print Dialog Box	Figure 1. Print dialog box

Capitalizing lists

For itemized lists, use sentence capitalization (Abc def). Lowercase (abc def) makes it difficult for users to see patterns (for example, alphabetical ordering) when scanning list items, and title capitalization (Abc Def) makes it difficult for them to distinguish between proper and non-proper nouns.

Change	To
This section describes the following:	This section describes the following:
▪ File Menu	▪ File menu
▪ Edit Menu	▪ Edit menu
▪ View Menu	▪ View menu

Capitalizing glossaries

For glossary terms that are not proper nouns, use lowercase (abc). Using uppercase (ABC DEF), title capitalization (Abc Def), or sentence capitalization (Abc def) adds visual noise to glossary terms.

Change	To

Modular writing
    Element-based writing method.
	modular writing
	    Element-based writing method.

SGML
    standard generalized markup language. Generic markup language used to represent documents.
	SGML
	    Standard Generalized Markup Language. Generic markup language used to represent documents.

Headings

For headings, answer specific questions as directly as possible. Use a consistent heading syntax that indicates the module type and exactly what information the module contains.

Answering questions

Use headings to answer specific questions directly.

Question	Heading
Who should use AcmePro?	Who should use AcmePro
What does AcmePro do?	What AcmePro does
When to upgrade AcmePro?	When to upgrade AcmePro
Where is the AcmePro executable?	Location of important files
Why should I use AcmePro?	Reasons for using AcmePro
How do I install AcmePro?	To install AcmePro

Labeling sections

When labeling document sections, use a consistent and predictable heading syntax that indicates what type information the section contains.

Information type	Heading syntax
Definitions	Types of dialog boxes
Definition 1	About the ABC dialog box
Definition 2	About the DEF dialog box
Procedures	Installing AcmePro
Procedure 1	To install AcmePro automatically
Procedure 2	To install AcmePro manually
Processes	Problem solving
Process 1	Detecting problems
Process 2	Investigating problems
Process 3	Solving problems
Process 4	Documenting solutions
Topics	About Acme Pro
Topic 1	Who should use AcmePro
Topic 2	What AcmePro does
Topic 3	Reasons for using AcmePro

Indexes

When indexing document sections, use a consistent and predictable syntax that indicates the type of information contained in the targeted section.

In user documentation, the two most common information types are procedures and topics:

- **Procedures**
  Step-by-step instructions that answer one question only: *How?*

- **Topics**
  Sections and subsections that answer any other question: *Who? What? When? Where? Why?*

Indexing procedures

Index procedures by noun and verb, using gerunds (that is, verbs ending in "ing") instead of the active form of the verb.

Section headings	Index entries
Printing	printing, 39–45
To print a document	document, printing, 39
	printing document, 39

Indexing topics

Index topics by noun. Begin each entry with the subject of the topic. End each with a single word indicating the question answered by the topic (*who*, *what*, *when*, *where*, or *why*).

Section headings	Index entries
About Acme AntiVirus	AcmePro
How Acme AntiVirus works	about, 7
Reasons for using Acme AntiVirus	how it works, 9–10
	why use, 8
When to scan drives	drives, when to scan, 39
Types of viruses	viruses, types, 27
If automatic protection fails	automatic protection failure, 89
	failure, automatic protection, 89
	protection failure, 89

Person

Person is the form of a personal pronoun indicating whether the pronoun represents the speaker (first person), the person spoken to (second person), or the person or thing spoken about (third person). Address your primary audience in second person singular (for example, "you"). Address your secondary audience in third person plural (for example, "administrators").

TIP: *To avoid awkward gender constructions, use plural for secondary audiences (for example, use "operators" instead of "the operator").*

Second person (primary audience)	Third person (secondary audience)
You can use runtime data and historical data to generate reports. Historical data can also be helpful when *you* create instructions to help operators solve problems caused by similar events.	*Administrators* can use runtime data and historical data to generate reports. Historical data can also be helpful when *administrators* create instructions to help operators solve problems caused by similar events.

Dysfunctional Documents

Sentences

In sentences, use parallel construction for words or phrases separated by commas or semicolons. Repeat "helper" words (for example, articles, conjunctions, prepositions, pronouns, and verbs) in each clause. To test parallel construction, convert sentences into itemized lists.

Change	To
As an operator, you can save console session settings and reload assigned defaults.	As an operator, you can save console session settings, and *you* can reload assigned defaults.
	As an operator, you can do the following: ■ Save console session settings. ■ Reload assigned defaults.

Tense

Users view documentation in real time. "Now" is wherever they are at the moment. To maintain this user-centered perspective, write in "eternal" present tense wherever possible. Write in past or future tense only when referring to something that occurs before or after the current phrase or sentence.

Change	To
After you have set up your printer, you can print a test document.	After you set up your printer, you can print a test document.

Change	To
After detecting a problem, you will be able to automatically highlight the affected node in the object pane.	After you detect a problem, you can automatically highlight the affected node in the object pane.

Voice

To speak clearly and directly to users, write phrases and sentences in active voice rather than passive voice.

Change	To
Duplicate message suppression works on the following principle: the event, for example a logfile entry, is compared with a condition.	AcmePro suppresses duplicate messages by comparing an event (for example, a logfile entry) with a condition.

Appendix D
Roles and responsibilities

All documentation team members—writers, editors, and managers—are responsible for the health of their user documents. Each team member has a specific role to play in collaboration, oversight, treatment, and prevention.

Collaborative writing guidelines are the key to document health. By working together to develop in-house guidelines, based on painfully honest document edits, teams can transform the negative cycles that produce dysfunctional documents into positive cycles that produce usable documents. Fully functional documents are a pleasure to develop—and use.

Collaboration roles

To improve collaboration, set up systematic edit cycles:

- **Writers**
  Do not just send documents out for technical or peer review. Send them out for edit as well.

- **Editors**
  Start conversations with writers before they begin to plan documents, not after they complete them.

- **Managers**
  Schedule edits of all documents. Encourage writers and editors to explain their respective points of view.

Oversight roles

To improve document oversight, assign key roles to the most experienced editors:

- **Writers**
  Treat editors as your first users. A second set of eyes can never hurt. Prepare to accept constructive criticism.

- **Editors**
  You are a service provider, not a policeman. Writers are your internal customers. Use diplomacy, not brute force.

- **Managers**
  Do not assign junior writers to "edit" the documents of senior writers. Assign experienced editors to thoroughly examine the documents of all writers.

Treatment roles

To treat document dysfunction, develop local solutions:

- **Writers**
  Do not throw the baby out with the bath. Just because a third-party blueprint of an ideal documentation set ended up in your bottom drawer does not mean that all cures are bad. It just means that top-down cures do not work.

- **Editors**
  Use edit reports to repair individual documents and style guidelines. Rebuild failed documents and guidelines, as needed. Remember, there are no shortcuts.

- **Managers**
  Base solutions on in-house experience, not external theory.
  Do not impose top-down solutions, particularly from third
  parties. Encourage bottom-up solutions from your own
  writers and editors.

Prevention roles

To prevent relapses of document dysfunction, develop
consensual writing guidelines:

- **Writers**
  Do not just complain about bad writing guidelines. Propose
  alternatives. Use editors as your advocates.

- **Editors**
  Do not just edit the document in front of you. Think ahead.
  Use individual edits to develop writing guidelines for the
  entire team. Become advocates for writers.

- **Managers**
  Do not appoint an ivory tower committee to rebrand a
  third-party style guide. Encourage writers and editors to
  develop a bottom-up style guide to meet local needs.

Dysfunctional Documents

References

[1] R. Van Buren and M. F. Buehler, The Levels of Edit, 2nd ed., Arlington: Society for Technical Communication, 1980.

[2] The University of Chicago, The Chicago Manual of Style, 16th ed., Chicago: The University of Chicago Press, 2010.

[3] K. Ament, Single Sourcing: Building Modular Documentation, New York: William Andrew Publishing, 2003.

[4] K. Ament, Indexing: A Nuts-and-Bolts Guide for Technical Writers, New York: William Andrew Publishing, 2001.

[5] W. Strunk Jr. and E. B. White, The Elements of Style, New York: Macmillan, 1988.

Dysfunctional Documents

Index

Dysfunctional Documents

T

U

Index

Made in the USA
Middletown, DE
17 May 2022